THE BEST
DOGS
EVER

CHIHUAHUAS ARE THE BEST!

Elaine Landau

⌐ LERNER PUBLICATIONS COMPANY · MINNEAPOLIS

For Shelly Glantz

Lerner Publications Company
A division of Lerner Publishing Group, Inc.
241 First Avenue North
Minneapolis, MN 55401 U.S.A.

Website address: www.lernerbooks.com

Library of Congress Cataloging-in-Publication Data

Landau, Elaine.
    Chihuahuas are the best! / by Elaine Landau.
       p.   cm. — (The best dogs ever)
    Includes index.
    ISBN 978-1-58013-567-2 (lib. bdg. : alk. paper)
    1. Chihuahua (Dog breed) I. Title.
  SF429.C45L36 2010
  636.76—dc22   2009012313

Manufactured in the United States of America
1 - BP - 12/15/09

TABLE OF CONTENTS

CHAPTER ONE

TINY AND TERRIFIC!

Do you think good things come in small packages?
Could a petite pooch with big eyes and ears win
your heart? Is a tiny dog with a huge personality
your kind of canine? If so, you might fall for a
Chihuahua—or Chi for short.

Being Petite Can Be Neat

Chis are the world's smallest dogs. You can fit one in your book bag. Most kids have teddy bears bigger than these pets.

PICKING A NAME

What's a good name for the world's smallest dog? There are lots of choices. Does one of these describe your Chi?

Munchkin

Pixie

Elf

HULK

Burly

BITS

Peanut

Bigfoot

BRAWNY

Ninja

A Chi stands about 5 inches (13 centimeters) high at the shoulder. That's shorter than a new pencil. Full-grown Chis only weigh between 4 and 6 pounds (2 and 3 kilograms).

Though all Chis are small, they don't all look alike. Some have short, smooth coats, while others have long coats. These dogs come in different colors too. Many are solid. Others have different colored markings.

Chis come in many colors, from brown to cream to gold.

A HOLLYWOOD FAVORITE

Hollywood stars have always loved Chis. Actresses Marilyn Monroe and Jayne Mansfield owned Chis. Present-day celebrities Paris Hilton (right), Hilary Duff, and Paula Abdul picked these dogs as pets as well.

Smart and Sassy

Chis are smart as well as cute. They can also be feisty and fearless. These dogs don't seem to know they're small. They are always ready and willing to protect their owners.

BOLD LITTLE WOOFERS

Chis don't quickly warm up to strangers. They may angrily bark at them instead. They aren't very fond of strange dogs either. Chis have taken on dogs more than twice their size. The Chi often does best with its own breed. That may be why many Chi owners have more than one of these spunky pint-sized canines.

Chis love being with their owners too. Their favorite spot is often their owner's lap. A Chi is happiest when it's being petted and cuddled. Chi owners are sure they have the best dogs ever.

CHAPTER TWO

FROM THEN TO NOW

The Chi's history is a bit of a mystery. Some think these dogs first came from China. Others say they came from Egypt.

Still others are sure Chis got their start in Mexico. Carvings of dogs like them have been found there. Some date back to the 800s. We know that Chis were in Mexico by the 1400s. Spanish explorers wrote home about them.

DRESS FOR SUCCESS

Many Chi owners like to dress up their dogs. All sorts of outfits are sold for these tiny pooches. There are ball gowns for girl dogs and Superman suits for boy dogs. There are even Chi fashion shows in different cities!

To the North

In the mid-1800s, Chis were brought to the United States. Americans visiting Mexico liked these little dogs. They took them home as pets.

Soon American breeders bred and sold them. Many won prizes in dog shows.

Handlers prepare four Chis for judging at a dog show in 1954.

DID YOU KNOW?

Some Chis work as hearing dogs. Hearing dogs help people who are deaf or who have trouble hearing. They alert their owners to sounds around them. They might nudge their owners if a smoke alarm goes off. Or they might jump up on their owners if a phone, doorbell, or alarm clock rings.

A Toy Dog

The American Kennel Club (AKC) groups dogs by breed. Some of the AKC's groups include the sporting group, the working group, and the herding group.

This German shepherd is in the herding group.

Springer spaniels, like this one, are in the sporting group.

This boxer belongs to the working group.

CHARMING CHIHUAHUAS ON THE BIG SCREEN

Some talented Chis are in show business. Have you seen the Disney movie *Beverly Hills Chihuahua*? In this film, a rich, pampered Chi named Chloe gets lost on a Mexican vacation. She has to find her way home with the help of her four new Latin canine pals.

Chis are in the toy group. Other dogs in the toy group are the pug and the shih tzu. Toy dogs don't all look alike. But all of them are small enough to sit on your lap.

CHAPTER THREE
IS A CHI RIGHT FOR YOU?

Who wouldn't want a Chi? These cute canines seem so perfect. Yet they are not right for everyone. Read on to see if a Chi is the pup for you.

A Little Exercise for a Little Dog

Do you dream of jogging and hiking for hours with your dog? If so, don't get a Chi. These tiny canines need much less exercise than large dogs.

Chis do well with fairly short daily walks. They'll also enjoy fetching balls you throw them. Just don't plan a two-day mountain hike with your pint-sized pal.

Chis can get all the exercise they need by simply running through your house or romping in the backyard.

A Warm Climate Is Best

Chis do best in warm, sunny places. They don't like very cold weather. Going out in the snow or rain is not their thing.

Your Chi will love to hang out with you at the beach or the park in the sunshine!

Chis often seek out sunny spots for their naps.

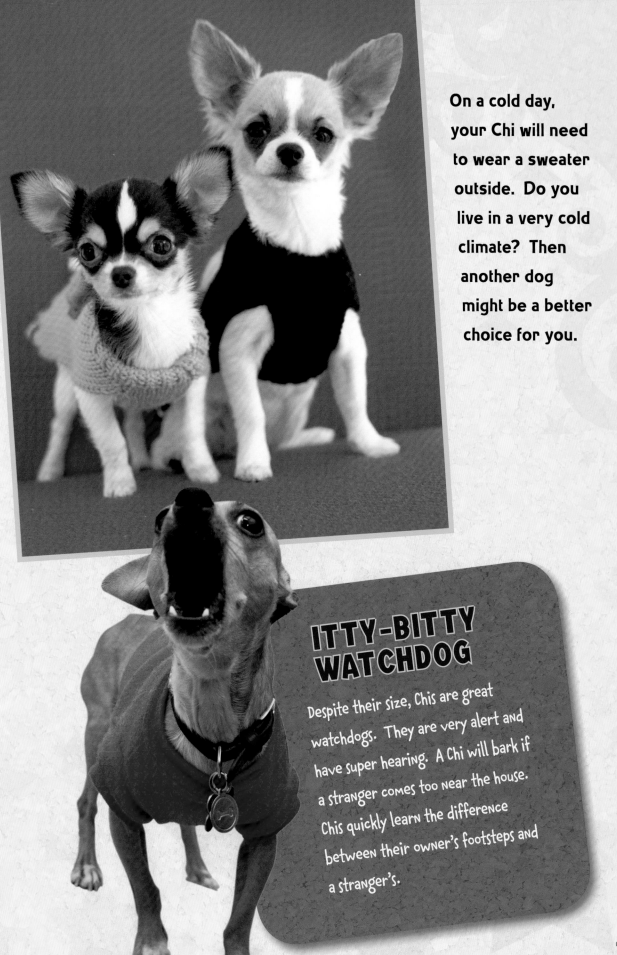

On a cold day, your Chi will need to wear a sweater outside. Do you live in a very cold climate? Then another dog might be a better choice for you.

ITTY-BITTY WATCHDOG

Despite their size, Chis are great watchdogs. They are very alert and have super hearing. A Chi will bark if a stranger comes too near the house. Chis quickly learn the difference between their owner's footsteps and a stranger's.

Do You Have Lots of Spare Time?

Chis become very close to their owners. Your Chi will dote on you. It will want to spend a lot of time with you.

Chis are not ideal pets for busy people. Are you out of the house a lot? Will your Chi be alone most of the day? Then think twice before getting a Chi.

A Chi can get lonely if it's left at home alone.

Yet if you have time for one, a Chi is a terrific dog. Chis seem to sense their owners' moods. They can be great company.

GOOD NEWS FOR CHIS

Chis have a really long life span. With good care, these dogs can live for eighteen years or longer. That's good news for Chis and their owners.

CHAPTER FOUR

THE BEST DAY EVER

Today is a great day. You've found the Chi you want.
Now you're going to bring your dog home.

You've picked out your new pup's name. You've told your friends about the dog. You feel ready to be a good dog owner.

Be sure to handle your new Chi gently. It's important to be careful with these tiny dogs.

Be Ready

Yet are you really ready? You'll need plenty of supplies to care for your new Chi. Not sure what you'll need to welcome Fido to your family? This basic list is a great place to start:

- crates (one for when your pet travels by car and one for it to rest in at home)

- tags (for identification)

- dog food

- collar

- leash

- food and water bowls

- treats (to be used in training)

- toys

Make sure the toys you buy for your Chi are the right size for a small dog.

Keep Your Dog Healthy

Veterinarians, or vets, are doctors who treat animals. Take your new Chi to a vet soon. A vet will give your dog the shots it needs. This is important for your Chi's health.

Your dog will need to go back to the vet for checkups. Be sure to also take your dog to the vet if it gets sick.

A vet will keep your Chi in good health.

Mealtime!

Ask your vet what to feed your Chi. Many Chis are picky eaters. You may have to try a few types of food.

Don't give your dog scraps from the table. Small dogs have small tummies. Your Chi will feel full and not eat its own food.

TASTY TREATS

Use dog treats as rewards when training your dog. Don't give your dog treats for dessert. You could end up with an overweight pooch.

Make Your Dog Feel at Home

Welcome your dog to the family. Spend extra time with it in the first week. Be sure to pet and play with your puppy a lot.

PROPER CARE

Brush your Chi every day. If you brush your Chi often, you will not need to bathe it as much. A bath every six weeks will usually be enough.

Most Chis love to play fetch. They are happy to chase after a small ball or stick. A gentle game of tug can be fun too. Most pet stores carry small toys for small dogs.

Friends to the End

Your Chi will become your new best friend. It will be loving and loyal. Be sure to take extra good care of this special pet.

Never forget to feed or walk your Chi. Spend time with your dog. Give it all the love you can. Make your Chi as happy as it makes you!

GLOSSARY

American Kennel Club (AKC): an organization that groups dogs by breed. The AKC also defines the characteristics of different breeds.

breed: a particular type of dog. Dogs of the same breed have the same body shape and general features. *Breed* can also refer to producing puppies.

breeder: someone who mates dogs to produce a particular type of dog

canine: a dog, or having to do with dogs

coat: a dog's fur

dote: to pay a lot of attention to or to show a great deal of affection for

feisty: very lively or frisky

hearing dog: a dog used to help people who have trouble hearing or who are deaf

petite: very small

toy group: a group of different types of dogs that are all small in size

veterinarian: a doctor who treats animals. Veterinarians are called vets for short.

FOR MORE INFORMATION

Books

Brecke, Nicole, and Patricia M. Stockland. *Dogs You Can Draw*. Minneapolis: Millbrook Press, 2010. Dog lovers can learn to draw many of their favorite breeds in this fun and colorful title.

Gray, Susan H. *Chihuahuas*. Chanhassen, MN: Child's World, 2007. This book includes lots of interesting information about Chihuahuas as well as cute photos of the dogs.

Landau, Elaine. *Your Pet Dog*. Rev. ed. New York: Children's Press, 2007. This title is a good guide for young people on choosing and caring for a dog.

Lunis, Natalie. *Chihuahua: Señor Tiny*. New York: Bearport, 2009. Learn more about the Chihuahua, and read true stories about these amazing dogs—including a tale of a Chihuahua who saved a baby from a rattlesnake!

Markle, Sandra. *Animal Heroes: True Rescue Stories*. Minneapolis: Millbrook Press, 2009. Markle describes how dogs and other animals have helped humans in dangerous situations.

Websites

American Kennel Club

http://www.akc.org

Visit this website to find a complete listing of AKC- registered dog breeds, including the Chihuahua. This site also features fun printable activities for kids.

ASPCA Animaland

http://www2.aspca.org/site/PageServer?pagename=kids_pc_home

Check out this page for helpful hints on caring for a dog and other pets.

Index

Photo Acknowledgments

The images in this book are used with the permission of: backgrounds © iStockphoto.com/Julie Fisher and © iStockphoto.com/Tomasz Adamczyk; © iStockphoto.com/Michael Balderas, pp. 1, 26 (top); © Jerry Shulman/SuperStock, pp. 4, 14 (bottom right); © Nikolai Pozdeev/Shutterstock Images, pp. 4-5; © Trinette Reed/Blend Images/Getty Images, p. 5; © BLOOMimage/Getty Images, pp. 6-7, 27; © Juniors Bildarchiv/Alamy, p. 7 (top); © Frank Trapper/CORBIS, p. 7 (bottom); © The Natural History Museum/Alamy, p. 8; © iStockphoto.com/Aldo Murillo, pp. 9, 17 (top); © iStockphoto.com/Marcin Pikula, p. 10; AP Photo/Kai-Uwe Knoth, p. 11 (top); © Eric Isselée/Dreamstime.com, p. 11 (bottom); © Fred Morley/Fox Photos/Hulton Archive/Getty Images, p. 12; © Willard R. Culver/National Geographic/Getty Images, p. 13 (top); © Andrey Medvedev/Dreamstime.com, p. 13 (bottom); © GK Hart/Vikki Hart/Photodisc/Getty Images, p. 14 (left); © SuperStock, Inc./SuperStock, p. 14 (top right); © Yamada Taro/Riser/Getty Images, p. 15; © Sharon Montrose/The Image Bank/Getty Images, p. 16; © iStockphoto.com/Tamara Bauer, p. 17 (bottom); © Erik Von Weber/The Image Bank/Getty Images, p. 18 (left); © Jian Qiang Lee/Dreamstime.com, p. 18 (right); © Shinya Sasaki/NEOVISION/Getty Images, p. 19 (top); © Eric Brown/Alamy, p. 19 (bottom); © American Images Inc/Digital Vision/Getty Images, p. 20 (top); © iStockphoto.com/Pamela Moore, pp. 20 (bottom), 28-29; © Phartisan/Dreamstime.com, p. 21; © iStockphoto.com/Kelly Richardson, p. 22; © iStockphoto.com/Eric Isselée, pp. 22-23; © Jeff J Mitchell/Getty Images, p. 23; © April Turner/Dreamstime.com, p. 24 (top); © Tammy Mcallister/Dreamstime.com, p. 24 (center); © iStockphoto.com/Jill Fromer, p. 24 (bottom); © GK Hart/Vikki Hart/Taxi/Getty Images, p. 25; © Yves Lanceau/NHPA/Photoshot, p. 26 (bottom); © shootnikonrawstock/Alamy, p. 28; © LaCoppola-Meier/Photonica/Getty Images, p. 29.

Front Cover: © Larry Lilac/Alamy.
Back Cover: © Nikolai Pozdeev/Shutterstock Images.